The Key Facts™
on Iran

Essential Information on Iran
By Patrick W. Nee

The Internationalist®
www.internationalist.com

The Internationalist®

International Business, Investment, and Travel

Published by:

The Internationalist Publishing Company

96 Walter Street/ Suite 200

Boston, MA 02131, USA

Tel: 617-354-7722

www.internationalist.com

PN@internationalist.com

Table Of Contents

Chapter 1: Background:

Known as Persia until 1935, Iran became an Islamic
republic in 1979 after the ruling monarchy was
overthrown and Shah Mohammad Reza PAHLAVI was
forced into exile. Conservative clerical forces established
a theocratic system of government with ultimate political
authority vested in a learned religious scholar referred to
commonly as the Supreme Leader who, according to the
constitution, is accountable only to the Assembly of
Experts - a popularly elected 86-member body of clerics.
US-Iranian relations have been strained since a group of
Iranian students seized the US Embassy in Tehran on 4
November 1979 and held embassy personnel hostages
until 20 January 1981. The US cut off diplomatic
relations with Iran in April 1980. During the period
1980-88, Iran fought a bloody, indecisive war with Iraw
that eventually expanded into the Persian gulf and led to
clashes between US Navy and Iranian military forces.
Iran has been dseignated as tate sponsor of terrorism for
its activities in Lebanon and elsewhere in the world and
remains subject to US, UN, and EU economic sanctions
and export controls because of its continued involvement
in terrorism and concerns over possible military
dimensions of its nuclear program. Following the lection
of reformer Johhat ol-Eslam Mohammad KHATAMI as
president in 1997 and a reformist Majles (legislature) in
2000, a campaign to foster politica reform in response to
popular dissatisfaction was initiated. The movement
floundered as the security services reversed and blocked
reform measures while increasing security repression.
Starting with nationwide municipal elections in 2003

and continuing through Majles elections in 2004, conservatives reestablished control over Iran's elected government institutions, which culminated with the August 2005 inauguration of hardliner Mahmud AHMADI-NEJAD as president. His controversial reelection in June 2009 sparked nationwide protests over allegations of electoral fraud. these protests were quickly suppressed,a nd the political opposition that arouse as a consequence of AHMADI-NEJAD's election was at least two major economically based protests in July and October 2012, but Iran's internal security situation remained stable. President AHMADI-NEJAD's independent streak angered regime establishment figures, including the Supreme Leader, leading to conservative opposition to his agenda fro the last year of his presidency, and an alienation of his political supporters. In June 2013 iranians elected a mdoerate conservative cleric, Dr. Hasan Fereidun RUHANI to the presidency. He is a long-time senior member in the regime, but has made promises of reforming soceity and Iran's foreign policy. The UN Security Council has passed a number of resolutions calling for Iran to suspend its uranium enrichment and reprocessing activities and comply with its IAEA obligations and responsibilities, but in November 2013 the five permanent members, plus Germany, (P5+1) signed a joint plan with Iran to provide the country with incremental relief from international pressure for positive steps towards transparency of their nuclear program.

Chapter 2: Geography

Location:

> Middle East, bordering the Gulf of Oman, the Persian Gulf, and the Caspian Sea, between Iraq and Pakistan

Geographic coordinates:

> 32 00 N, 53 00 E

Map references:

> Middle East

Area:

> total: 1,648,195 sq km
>
> country comparison to the world: 18
>
> land: 1,531,595 sq km
>
> water: 116,600 sq km

Area - comparative:

> slightly smaller than Alaska

Land boundaries:

> total: 5,440 km
>
> border countries: Afghanistan 936 km, Armenia 35 km, Azerbaijan-proper 432 km, Azerbaijan-Naxcivan exclave 179 km, Iraq 1,458 km, Pakistan 909 km, Turkey 499 km, Turkmenistan 992 km

Coastline:

2,440 km; note - Iran also borders the Caspian Sea (740 km)

Maritime claims:

territorial sea: 12 nm

contiguous zone: 24 nm

exclusive economic zone: bilateral agreements or median lines in the Persian Gulf

continental shelf: natural prolongation

Climate:

mostly arid or semiarid, subtropical along Caspian coast

Terrain:

rugged, mountainous rim; high, central basin with deserts, mountains; small, discontinuous plains along both coasts

Elevation extremes:

lowest point: Caspian Sea -28 m

highest point: Kuh-e Damavand 5,671 m

Natural resources:

petroleum, natural gas, coal, chromium, copper, iron ore, lead, manganese, zinc, sulfur

Land use:

arable land: 10.05%

permanent crops: 1.08%

other: 88.86% (2011)

Irrigated land:

87,000 sq km (2009)

Total renewable water resources:

137 cu km (2011)

Freshwater withdrawal (domestic/industrial/agricultural):

total: 93.3 cu km/yr (7%/1%/92%)

per capita: 1,306 cu m/yr (2004)

Natural hazards:

periodic droughts, floods; dust storms, sandstorms; earthquakes

Environment - current issues:

air pollution, especially in urban areas, from vehicle emissions, refinery operations, and industrial effluents; deforestation; overgrazing; desertification; oil pollution in the Persian Gulf; wetland losses from drought; soil degradation (salination); inadequate supplies of potable water; water pollution from raw sewage and industrial waste; urbanization

Environment - international agreements:

party to: Biodiversity, Climate Change, Climate Change-Kyoto Protocol, Desertification, Endangered Species, Hazardous Wastes, Marine Dumping, Ozone Layer Protection, Ship Pollution, Wetlands

<u>signed, but not ratified</u>: Environmental Modification, Law of the Sea, Marine Life Conservation

Geography - note:

strategic location on the Persian Gulf and Strait of Hormuz, which are vital maritime pathways for crude oil transport

Chapter 3: People and Society

Nationality:

 <u>noun</u>: Iranian(s)

 <u>adjective</u>: Iranian

Ethnic groups:

 Persian 61%, Azeri 16%, Kurd 10%, Lur 6%, Baloch 2%, Arab 2%, Turkmen and Turkic tribes 2%, other 1%

Languages:

 Persian (official) 53%, Azeri Turkic and Turkic dialects 18%, Kurdish 10%, Gilaki and Mazandarani 7%, Luri 6%, Balochi 2%, Arabic 2%, other 2%

Religions:

 Muslim (official) 98% (Shia 89%, Sunni 9%), other (includes Zoroastrian, Jewish, Christian, and Baha'i) 2%

Population:

 80,840,713 (July 2014 est.)

 <u>country comparison to the world</u>: 19

Age structure:

 <u>0-14 years</u>: 23.7% (male 9,834,866/female 9,350,017)

 <u>15-24 years</u>: 18.7% (male 7,757,256/female 7,341,309)

25-54 years: 46.1% (male 18,955,874/female 18,289,849)

55-64 years: 6.3% (male 2,519,630/female 2,603,458)

65 years and over: 5.1% (male 1,941,692/female 2,246,762) (2014 est.)

Median age:

total: 28.3 years

male: 28 years

female: 28.6 years (2014 est.)

Population growth rate:

1.22% (2014 est.)

country comparison to the world: 97

Birth rate:

18.52 births/1,000 population (2014 est.)

country comparison to the world: 105

Death rate:

5.94 deaths/1,000 population (2014 est.)

country comparison to the world: 168

Net migration rate:

-0.08 migrant(s)/1,000 population (2014 est.)

country comparison to the world: 115

Urbanization:

urban population: 69.1% of total population (2011)

rate of urbanization: 1.25% annual rate of change (2010-15 est.)

Major cities - population:

TEHRAN (capital) 7.304 million; Mashhad 2.713 million; Esfahan 1.781 million; Karaj 1.635 million; Tabriz 1.509 million; Shiraz 1.321 million (2011)

Sex ratio:

at birth: 1.05 male(s)/female

under 15 years: 1.05 male(s)/female

15-64 years: 1.03 male(s)/female

65 years and over: 0.89 male(s)/female

total population: 1.03 male(s)/female (2014 est.)

Maternal mortality rate:

21 deaths/100,000 live births (2010)

country comparison to the world: 137

Infant mortality rate:

total: 39 deaths/1,000 live births

country comparison to the world: 55

male: 39.53 deaths/1,000 live births

female: 38.45 deaths/1,000 live births (2014 est.)

Life expectancy at birth:

total population: 70.89 years

country comparison to the world: 148

male: 69.32 years

female: 72.53 years (2014 est.)

Total fertility rate:

1.85 children born/woman (2014 est.)

country comparison to the world: 146

Health expenditures:

6% of GDP (2011)

country comparison to the world: 110

Physicians density:

0.89 physicians/1,000 population (2005)

Hospital bed density:

1.7 beds/1,000 population (2009)

Sanitation facility access:

improved:

urban: 97.7% of population

rural: 91.7% of population

total: 95.9% of population

unimproved:

urban: 2.3% of population

rural: 8.3% of population

total: 4.1% of population (2012 est.)

HIV/AIDS - adult prevalence rate:

0.2% (2012 est.)

country comparison to the world: 102

HIV/AIDS - people living with HIV/AIDS:

70,900 (2012 est.)

country comparison to the world: 54

HIV/AIDS - deaths:

4,600 (2012 est.)

country comparison to the world: 54

Major infectious diseases:

degree of risk: intermediate

food or waterborne diseases: bacterial diarrhea

vectorborne diseases: Crimean Congo hemorrhagic fever and malaria

note: highly pathogenic H5N1 avian influenza has been identified in this country; it poses a negligible risk with extremely rare cases possible among US citizens who have close contact with birds (2013)

Obesity - adult prevalence rate:

19.4% (2008)

country comparison to the world: 99

Education expenditures:

3.7% of GDP (2012)

country comparison to the world: 119

Literacy:

definition: age 15 and over can read and write

total population: 85%

male: 89.3%

female: 80.7% (2008 est.)

School life expectancy (primary to tertiary education):

total: 15 years

male: 15 years

female: 15 years (2012)

Unemployment, youth ages 15-24:

total: 23%

country comparison to the world: 48

male: 20.2%

female: 33.9% (2008)

Chapter 4: Government

Country name:

> conventional long form: Islamic Republic of Iran

> conventional short form: Iran

> local long form: Jomhuri-ye Eslami-ye Iran

> local short form: Iran

> former: Persia

Government type:

> theocratic republic

Capital:

> name: Tehran

> geographic coordinates: 35 42 N, 51 25 E

> time difference: UTC+3.5 (8.5 hours ahead of Washington, DC during Standard Time)

> daylight saving time: +1hr, begins fourth Tuesday in March; ends fourth Thursday in September

Administrative divisions:

> 31 provinces (ostanha, singular - ostan); Alborz, Ardabil, Azarbayjan-e Gharbi (West Azerbaijan), Azarbayjan-e Sharqi (East Azerbaijan), Bushehr, Chahar Mahal va Bakhtiari, Esfahan, Fars, Gilan, Golestan, Hamadan,

Hormozgan, Ilam, Kerman, Kermanshah, Khorasan-e Jonubi (South Khorasan), Khorasan-e Razavi (Razavi Khorasan), Khorasan-e Shomali (North Khorasan), Khuzestan, Kohgiluyeh va Bowyer Ahmad, Kordestan, Lorestan, Markazi, Mazandaran, Qazvin, Qom, Semnan, Sistan va Baluchestan, Tehran, Yazd, Zanjan

Independence:

1 April 1979 (Islamic Republic of Iran proclaimed); notable earlier dates: ca. 625 B.C. (unification of Iran under the Medes); ca. A.D. 1501 (Iran reunified under the Safavids); 12 December 1925 (modern Iran established under the Pahlavis)

National holiday:

Republic Day, 1 April (1979)

Constitution:

previous 1906; latest adopted 24 October 1979, effective 3 December 1979; amended 1989 (2013)

Legal system:

religious legal system based on sharia law

International law organization participation:

has not submitted an ICJ jurisdiction declaration; non-party state to the ICCt

Suffrage:

18 years of age; universal

Executive branch:

chief of state: Supreme Leader Ali Hoseini-KHAMENEI (since 4 June 1989)

head of government: President Mahmud AHMADI-NEJAD (since 3 August 2005); First Vice President Mohammad Reza RAHIMI (since 13 September 2009)

cabinet: Council of Ministers selected by the president with legislative approval; the Supreme Leader has some control over appointments to the more sensitive ministries

note: also considered part of the Executive branch of government are three oversight bodies: 1) Assembly of Experts (Majles-e Khoebregan), a popularly elected body charged with determining the succession of the Supreme Leader, reviewing his performance, and deposing him if deemed necessary; 2) Expediency Council or the Council for the Discernment of Expediency (Majma-ye- Tashkhis-e -Maslahat-e- Nezam) exerts supervisory authority over the executive, judicial, and legislative branches and resolves legislative issues when the Majles and the Council of Guardians disagree and since 1989 has been used to advise national religious leaders on matters of national policy; in 2005 the Council's powers were expanded to act as a supervisory body for the government; 3) Council of Guardians of the Constitution or Council of Guardians or Guardians Council (Shora-ye Negban-e Qanon-e Asasi) determines whether proposed legislation is both constitutional and faithful to Islamic law, vets candidates in popular elections for suitability, and supervises national elections

elections: supreme leader appointed for life by the Assembly of Experts; president elected by popular vote for a four-year term (eligible for a second terma nd additional nonconsecutive term); election last held on 14 June 2013 (next presidential election to be held ni June 2017)

election results: Hasan fereidun RUHANI 50.7%, Mohammad Baqer QALIBAF 16.5%, Saeed JALILI 11.4%, Mohsen REZAI 10.6%, Ali Akber VELAYATI 6.2%, other 4.6%

Legislative branch:

unicameral Islamic Consultative Assembly or Majles-e Shura-ye Eslami or Majles (290 seats; members elected by popular vote from single and multimember districts to serve four-year terms)

elections: last held on 2 March 2012 (first round); second round held on 4 May 2012; (next election to be held in 2016)

election results: percent of vote by party - NA; seats by party - NA

Judicial branch:

The Supreme Court (Qeveh Qazaieh) and the four-member High Council of the Judiciary have a single head and overlapping responsibilities; together they supervise the enforcement of all laws and establish judicial and legal policies; lower courts include a special clerical court, a revolutionary court, and a special administrative court

Political parties and leaders:

Note: formal political parties are a relatively new phenomenon in Iran and most conservatives still prefer to work through political pressure groups rather than parties; often political parties or coalitions are formed prior to elections and disbanded soon thereafter; a loose pro-reform coalition called the 2nd Khordad Front, which includes political parties as well as less formal groups and organizations, achieved considerable success in elections for the sixth Majles in early 2000; groups in the coalition included the Islamic Iran Participation Front (IIPF), Executives of Construction Party (Kargozaran), Solidarity Party, Islamic Labor Party, Mardom Salari, Mojahedin of the Islamic Revolution Organization (MIRO), and Militant Clerics Society (MCS; Ruhaniyun); the coalition participated in the seventh Majles elections in early 2004 but boycotted them after 80 incumbent reformists were disqualified; following his defeat in the 2005 presidential elections, former MCS Secretary General and sixth Majles Speaker Mehdi KARUBI formed the National Trust Party; a new conservative group, Islamic Iran Developers Coalition (Abadgaran), took a leading position in the new Majles after winning a majority of the seats in February 2004; ahead of the 2008 Majles elections, traditional and hardline conservatives attempted to close ranks under the United Front of Principlists and the Broad Popular Coalition of Principlists; several reformist groups, such as the MIRO and the IIPF, also came together as a reformist coalition in advance of the 2008 Majles elections; the IIPF has repeatedly complained that the overwhelming majority of its candidates were unfairly disqualified from the 2008 elections

Political pressure groups and leaders:

groups that generally support the Islamic Republic: Ansar-e Hizballah-; Followers of the Line of the Imam and the Leader; Islamic Coalition Party (Motalefeh); Islamic Engineers Society; Tehran Militant Clergy Association (MCA; Ruhaniyat)

active pro-reform student group: Office of Strengthening Unity (OSU)

opposition groups: Freedom Movement of Iran; Green Path movement [Mehdi KARUBI, Mir-Hosein MUSAVI]; Marz-e Por Gohar; National Front; various ethnic and monarchist organizations

armed political groups repressed by the government: Democratic Party of Iranian Kurdistan (KDPI); Harekat-e Ansar-e Iran (splinter faction of Jundallah); Jaysh I-Adl (formerly known as Jundallah); Komala; Mojahedin-e Khalq Organization (MEK or MKO); People's Fedayeen; People's Free Life Party of Kurdistan (PJAK)

International organization participation:

CICA, CP, D-8, ECO, FAO, G-15, G-24, G-77, IAEA, IBRD, ICAO, ICC (national committees), ICRM, IDA, IDB, IFAD, IFC, IFRCS, IHO, ILO, IMF, IMO, IMSO, Interpol, IOC, IOM, IPU, ISO, ITSO, ITU, MIGA, NAM, OIC, OPCW, OPEC, PCA, SAARC (observer), SCO (observer), UN, UNAMID, UNCTAD, UNESCO,

UNHCR, UNIDO, UNITAR, UNWTO, UPU, WCO, WFTU (NGOs), WHO, WIPO, WMO, WTO (observer)

Diplomatic representation in the US:

none; note - Iran has an Interests Section in the Pakistani Embassy; address: Iranian Interests Section, Pakistani Embassy, 2209 Wisconsin Avenue NW, Washington, DC 20007; telephone: [1] (202) 965-4990; FAX [1] (202) 965-1073

Diplomatic representation from the US:

none; note - the US Interests Section is located in the Embassy of Switzerland No. 39 Shahid Mousavi (Golestan 5th), Pasdaran Ave., Tehran, Iran; telephone [98] 21 2254 2178/2256 5273; FAX [98] 21 2258 0432

Key Leaders of Iran

Supreme Leader	**Ali Hoseini-KHAMENEI,** *Ayatollah*
Pres.	**Hasan Fereidun RUHANI,** *Hojjat ol-Eslam*
Sec. of the Cabinet	**Mohsen HAJI-MIRZAIE**
Head, Presidential Office	**Mohammad NAHAVANDIAN**
First Vice Pres.	**Eshaq JAHANGIRI**

Vice Pres. & Head, Atomic Energy Organization of Iran	**Ali Akbar SALEHI**
Vice Pres. & Head, Cultural Heritage, Handicrafts, & Tourism	**Masud SOLTANIFAR**
Vice Pres. & Head, Environmental Protection Organization	**Masumeh EBTEKAR**
Vice Pres. for Executive Affairs	**Mohammad SHARIAT-MADARI**
Vice Pres. for Women's & Family Affairs	**Majid ANSARI,** *Hojjat ol-Eslam*
Vice Pres. for Legal Affairs	**Elham AMINZADEH**
Vice Pres. for Management, Development, & Human Resources	**Mohamad Baqer NOBAKHT**

Vice Pres. & Head, Martyrs & War Veterans Affairs Foundation	**Mohammad Ali SHAHIDI,** *Hojjat ol-Eslam*
Vice Pres. for Parliamentary Affairs	**Majid ANSARI,** *Hojjat ol-Eslam*
Vice Pres. for Planning & Strategic Supervision	**Mohammad Baqer NOBAKHT**
Vice Pres. for Scientific & Technological Affairs	**Sorena SATARI-Khavas**
Min. of Agricultural Jihad	**Mohammad HOJJATI**
Min. of Communication & Information Technology	**Mahmud VAEZI-Jazai**
Min. of Defense & Armed Forces Logistics	**Hosein DEHQAN**
Min. of Economic	**Ali TAYEB-NIA**

Affairs & Finance	
Min. of Education	**Ali Asqar FANI**
Min. of Energy	**Hamid CHITCHIAN**
Min. of Foreign Affairs	**Mohammad Javad ZARIF-Khonsari**
Min. of Health, Treatment, & Medical Education (Acting)	**Hasan QAZIZADEH-Hashemi**
Min. of Industry, Mining, & Trade	**Mohammad Reza NEMATZADEH**
Min. of Intelligence & Security	**Mahmud ALAVI-Tabar;** *Hojjat ol-Eslam*
Min. of Interior	**Abdolreza Rahmani-FAZLI**
Min. of Justice	**Mostafa PUR-MOHAMMADI,** *Hojjat ol-Eslam*
Min. of Labor, Cooperatives, & Social Welfare (Acting)	**Ali RABIEI**

Min. of Petroleum	**Bijan Namdar-ZANGANEH**
Min. of Roads & Urban Development	**Abbas Ahmad AKHUNDI**
Min. of Science, Research, & Technology	**Mohammad FARHADI**
Min. of Sports & Youth	**Mahmud GUDARZI**
Governor, Central Bank of Iran	**Valiollah SEIF**
Permanent Representative to the UN, New York	**Mohammad KHAZAI-Torshizi**

Flag description:

three equal horizontal bands of green (top), white, and red; the national emblem (a stylized representation of the word Allah in the shape of a tulip, a symbol of martyrdom) in red is centered in the white band; ALLAH AKBAR (God is Great) in white Arabic script is repeated 11 times along the bottom edge of the green band and 11 times along the top edge of the red band; green is the color of Islam and also represents growth,

white symbolizes honesty and peace, red stands for
bravery and martyrdom

National symbol(s):

lion

National anthem:

name: "Soroud-e Melli-ye Jomhouri-ye Eslami-ye Iran"
(National Anthem of the Islamic Republic of Iran)

lyrics/music: multiple authors/Hassan RIAHI

note: adopted 1990

Chapter 5: Economy

Economy - overview:

Iran's economy is marked by statist policies, an inefficient state sector, and reliance on oil, a major source of government revenues. Price controls, subsidies, and other distortions weigh down the economy, undermining the potential for private-sector-led growth. Private sector activity is typically limited to small-scale workshops, farming, some manufacturing, and services. Significant informal market activity flourishes and corruption is widespread. New fiscal and monetary constraints on Tehran, following the expansion of international sanctions in 2012 against Iran's Central Bank and oil exports, significantly reduced Iran's oil revenue, forced government spending cuts, and fueled a 60% currency depreciation. Economic growth turned negative in 2012 and 2013, for the first time in two decades. Iran continues to suffer from double-digit unemployment and underemployment. Lack of job opportunities has convinced many educated Iranian youth to seek jobs overseas, resulting in a significant "brain drain." However, the election of President Hasan RUHANI in June 2013 brought about widespread expectations of economic improvements and greater international engagement among the Iranian public, and early in Ruhani's term the country saw a strengthened national currency and a historic boost to market values at the Tehran stock exchange.

GDP (purchasing power parity):

$987.1 billion (2013 est.)

country comparison to the world: 19

$1.002 trillion (2012 est.)

$1.021 trillion (2011 est.)

note: data in 2013 US dollars

GDP (official exchange rate):

$411.9 billion (2013 est.)

GDP - real growth rate:

-1.5% (2013 est.)

country comparison to the world: 208

-1.9% (2012 est.)

3% (2011 est.)

GDP - per capita (PPP):

$12,800 (2013 est.)

country comparison to the world: 103

$13,200 (2012 est.)

$13,600 (2011est.)

note: data are in 2013 US dollars

GDP - composition by sector:

agriculture: 10.6%

industry: 44.9%

services: 44.5% (2013 est.)

Labor force:

27.72 million

country comparison to the world: 23

note: shortage of skilled labor (2013 est.)

Labor force - by occupation:

agriculture: 16.9%

industry: 34.4%

services: 48.7% (2012 est.)

Unemployment rate:

16% (2013 est.)

country comparison to the world: 142

15.5% (2012 est.)

note: data are according to the Iranian Government

Population below poverty line:

18.7% (2007 est.)

Household income or consumption by percentage share:

lowest 10%: 2.6%

highest 10%: 29.6% (2005)

Distribution of family income - Gini index:

44.5 (2006)

country comparison to the world: 45

Investment (gross fixed):

31.1% of GDP (2013 est.)

Budget:

revenues: $47.84 billion

expenditures: $66.38 billion (2013 est.)

Taxes and other revenues:

11.6% of GDP (2013 est.)

country comparison to the world: 160

Budget surplus (+) or deficit (-):

-4.5% of GDP (2013 est.)

country comparison to the world: 160

Public debt:

18.7% of GDP (2013 est.)

country comparison to the world: 137

18.6% of GDP (2012 est.)

note: includes publicly guaranteed debt

Inflation rate (consumer prices):

42.3% (2013 est.)

country comparison to the world: 221

30.5% (2012 est.)

note: official Iranian estimate

Commercial bank prime lending rate:

12% (2013 est.)

country comparison to the world: 74

11% (31 December 2012 est.)

Stock of narrow money:

$26.3 billion (31 December 2013 est.)

country comparison to the world: 62

$42.91 billion (31 December 2012 est.)

Stock of broad money:

$65.02 billion (31 December 2013 est.)

country comparison to the world: 65

$104.6 billion (31 December 2011 est.)

Stock of domestic credit:

$42.32 billion (31 December 2013 est.)

country comparison to the world: 63

$77.74 billion (31 December 2012 est.)

Market value of publicly traded shares:

$NA (31 December 2013 est.)

country comparison to the world: 34

$140.8 billion (31 December 2012)

$107.2 billion (31 December 2011)

Agriculture - products:

wheat, rice, other grains, sugar beets, sugarcane, fruits, nuts, cotton; dairy products, wool; caviar

Industries:

petroleum, petrochemicals, fertilizers, caustic soda, textiles, cement and other construction materials, food processing (particularly sugar refining and vegetable oil production), ferrous and non-ferrous metal fabrication, armaments

Industrial production growth rate:

-5.2% (2013 est.)

country comparison to the world: 191

Current account balance:

-$8.659 billion (2013 est.)

country comparison to the world: 174

-$9.333 billion (2012 est.)

Exports:

$61.22 billion (2013 est.)

country comparison to the world: 53

$67.04 billion (2012 est.)

Exports - commodities:

petroleum 80%, chemical and petrochemical products, fruits and nuts, carpets

Exports - partners:

China 22.1%, India 11.9%, Turkey 10.6%, South Korea 7.6%, Japan 7.1% (2012)

Imports:

$64.42 billion (2013 est.)

country comparison to the world: 46

$70.03 billion (2012 est.)

Imports - commodities:

industrial supplies, capital goods, foodstuffs and other consumer goods, technical services

Imports - partners:

UAE 33.2%, China 13.8%, Turkey 11.8%, South Korea 7.4% (2012)

Reserves of foreign exchange and gold:

$68.06 billion (31 December 2013 est.)

country comparison to the world: 32

$74.06 billion (31 December 2012 est.)

Debt - external:

$15.64 billion (2013 est.)

country comparison to the world: 87

$17.25 billion (31 December 2012 est.)

Stock of direct foreign investment - at home:

$41.45 billion (31 December 2013 est.)

country comparison to the world: 56

$37.31 billion (31 December 2012 est.)

Stock of direct foreign investment - abroad:

$3.645 billion (31 December 2013 est.)

country comparison to the world: 65

$3.345 billion (31 December 2012 est.)

Exchange rates:

Iranian rials (IRR) per US dollar -

18,517.2 (2013 est.)

12,175.5 (2012 est.)

10,254.18 (2010 est.)

9,864.3 (2009)

9,142.8 (2008)

note: Iran devalued its currency in July 2013

Fiscal year:

21 March - 20 March

Chapter 6: Energy

Electricity - production:

> 239.7 billion kWh (2011 est.)
>
> country comparison to the world: 18

Electricity - consumption:

> 199.8 billion kWh (2011 est.)
>
> country comparison to the world: 19

Electricity - exports:

> 6.707 billion kWh (2010 est.)
>
> country comparison to the world: 25

Electricity - imports:

> 3.015 billion kWh (2010 est.)
>
> country comparison to the world: 45

Electricity - installed generating capacity:

> 62.09 million kW (2010 est.)
>
> country comparison to the world: 15

Electricity - from fossil fuels:

> 86.2% of total installed capacity (2010 est.)
>
> country comparison to the world: 87

Electricity - from nuclear fuels:

0% of total installed capacity (2010 est.)

country comparison to the world: 109

Electricity - from hydroelectric plants:

13.7% of total installed capacity (2010 est.)

country comparison to the world: 104

Electricity - from other renewable sources:

0.2% of total installed capacity (2010 est.)

country comparison to the world: 96

Crude oil - production:

3.594 million bbl/day (2012 est.)

country comparison to the world: 6

Crude oil - exports:

2.445 million bbl/day (2011 est.)

country comparison to the world: 3

Crude oil - imports:

15,600 bbl/day (1 January 2013 est.)

country comparison to the world: 171

Crude oil - proved reserves:

154.6 billion bbl (1 January 2013 est.)

country comparison to the world: 4

Refined petroleum products - production:

1.718 million bbl/day (2011est.)

country comparison to the world: 12

Refined petroleum products - consumption:

1.709 million bbl/day (2012 est.)

country comparison to the world: 14

Refined petroleum products - exports:

330,800 bbl/day (2010 est.)

country comparison to the world: 21

Refined petroleum products - imports:

180,400 bbl/day (2010 est.)

country comparison to the world: 29

Natural gas - production:

162.6 billion cu m (2010 est.)

country comparison to the world: 4

Natural gas - consumption:

144.6 billion cu m (2010 est.)

country comparison to the world: 5

Natural gas - exports:

9.05 billion cu m (2011 est.)

country comparison to the world: 26

Natural gas - imports:

10.59 billion cu m (2011est.)

country comparison to the world: 29

Natural gas - proved reserves:

33.61 trillion cu m (1 January 2013 est.)

country comparison to the world: 2

Carbon dioxide emissions from consumption of energy:

624.9 million Mt (2011 est.)

Chapter 7: Communications

Telephones - main lines in use:

28.76 million (2012)

country comparison to the world: 12

Telephones - mobile cellular:

58.16 million (2012)

country comparison to the world: 24

Telephone system:

general assessment: currently being modernized and expanded with the goal of not only improving the efficiency and increasing the volume of the urban service but also bringing telephone service to several thousand villages, not presently connected

domestic: the addition of new fiber cables and modern switching and exchange systems installed by Iran's state-owned telecom company have improved and expanded the fixed-line network greatly; fixed-line availability has more than doubled to more than 27 million lines since 2000; additionally, mobile-cellular service has increased dramatically serving roughly 56 million subscribers in 2011; combined fixed and mobile-cellular subscribership now exceeds 100 per 100 persons

international: country code - 98; submarine fiber-optic cable to UAE with access to Fiber-Optic Link Around the Globe (FLAG); Trans-Asia-Europe (TAE) fiber-optic line runs from Azerbaijan through the northern portion of Iran to Turkmenistan with expansion to Georgia and Azerbaijan; HF radio and microwave radio relay to Turkey, Azerbaijan, Pakistan, Afghanistan, Turkmenistan, Syria, Kuwait, Tajikistan, and Uzbekistan; satellite earth stations - 13 (9 Intelsat and 4 Inmarsat)

Broadcast media:

state-run broadcast media with no private, independent broadcasters; Islamic Republic of Iran Broadcasting (IRIB), the state-run TV broadcaster, operates 5 nationwide channels, a news channel, about 30 provincial channels, and several international channels; about 20 foreign Persian-language TV stations broadcasting on satellite TV are capable of being seen in Iran; satellite dishes are illegal and, while their use had been tolerated, authorities began confiscating satellite dishes following the unrest stemming from the 2009 presidential election; IRIB operates 8 nationwide radio networks, a number of provincial stations, and an external service; most major international broadcasters transmit to Iran (2009)

Internet country code:

.ir

Internet hosts:

197,804 (2012)

country comparison to the world: 72

Internet users:

8.214 million (2009)

country comparison to the world: 35

Chapter 8: Transportation

Airports:

>319 (2013)

>country comparison to the world: 22

Airports - with paved runways:

>total: 140

>over 3,047 m: 42

>2,438 to 3,047 m: 29

>1,524 to 2,437 m: 26

>914 to 1,523 m: 36

>under 914 m: 7 (2013)

Airports - with unpaved runways:

>total: 179

>over 3,047 m: 1

>2,438 to 3,047 m: 2

>1,524 to 2,437 m: 9

>914 to 1,523 m: 135

>under 914 m: 32 (2013)

Heliports:

26 (2013)

Pipelines:

condensate 7 km; condensate/gas 973 km; gas 20,794 km; liquid petroleum gas 570 km; oil 8,625 km; refined products 7,937 km (2013)

Railways:

total: 8,442 km

country comparison to the world: 24

broad gauge: 94 km 1.676-m gauge

standard gauge: 8,348 km 1.435-m gauge (148 km electrified) (2008)

Roadways:

total: 198,866 km

country comparison to the world: 26

paved: 160,366 km (includes 1,948 km of expressways)

unpaved: 38,500 km (2010)

Waterways:

850 km (on Karun River; some navigation on Lake Urmia) (2012)

country comparison to the world: 70

Merchant marine:

total: 76

country comparison to the world: 60

by type: bulk carrier 8, cargo 51, chemical tanker 3, container 4, liquefied gas 1, passenger/cargo 3, petroleum tanker 2, refrigerated cargo 2, roll on/roll off 2

foreign-owned: 2 (UAE 2)

registered in other countries: 71 (Barbados 5, Cyprus 10, Hong Kong 3, Malta 48, Panama 5) (2010)

Ports and terminals:

Assaluyeh, Bandar Abbas, Bandar-e-Eman Khomeyni

Chapter 9: Military

Military branches:

Islamic Republic of Iran Regular Forces (Artesh):
Ground Forces, Navy, Air Force (IRIAF),
Khatemolanbia Air Defense Headquarters; Islamic
Revolutionary Guard Corps (Sepah-e Pasdaran-e
Enqelab-e Eslami, IRGC): Ground Resistance Forces,
Navy, Aerospace Force, Quds Force (special operations);
Law Enforcement Forces (2011)

Military service age and obligation:

19 years of age for compulsory military service; 16 years
of age for volunteers; 17 years of age for Law
Enforcement Forces; 15 years of age for Basij Forces
(Popular Mobilization Army); conscript military service
obligation - 18 months; women exempt from military
service (2008)

Manpower available for military service:

males age 16-49: 23,619,215

females age 16-49: 22,628,341 (2010 est.)

Manpower fit for military service:

males age 16-49: 20,149,222

females age 16-49: 19,417,275 (2010 est.)

Manpower reaching militarily significant age annually:

male: 715,111

female: 677,372 (2010 est.)

Military expenditures:

2.5% of GDP (2006)

country comparison to the world: 60

Chapter 10: Transnational Issues

Disputes - international:

Iran protests Afghanistan's limiting flow of dammed Helmand River tributaries during drought; Iraq's lack of a maritime boundary with Iran prompts jurisdiction disputes beyond the mouth of the Shatt al Arab in the Persian Gulf; Iran and UAE dispute Tunb Islands and Abu Musa Island, which are occupied by Iran; Azerbaijan, Kazakhstan, and Russia ratified Caspian seabed delimitation treaties based on equidistance, while Iran continues to insist on a one-fifth slice of the sea; Afghan and Iranian commissioners have discussed boundary monument densification and resurvey

Refugees and internally displaced persons:

refugees (country of origin): 43,268 (Iraq) (2013); 2.4 million (1 million registered, 1.4 million undocumented) (Afghanistan) (2014)

Trafficking in persons:

current situation: Iran is a presumed source, transit,a nd destination country for men, women, and children subjected to sex trafficking and forced labor; Iranian and Afghan boys and girls are forced into prostitution domestically; Iranian women are subjected to sex trafficking in Iran, Pakistan, the Persian gulf, and Europe; Azerbaijani women and children are also sexuallyexploited in Iran; Afghan migrants and refugees and Pakistani men and women are subjected to conditions of forced labor in Iran; NGO reports indicate that criminal organizations play a significant role in human trafficking in Iran.

tier rating: Tier 3 - Iran does not comply with the minimum standards for the elimination of trafficking, and is not making significant efforts to do so; the government does not share information on its anti-trafficking efforts, making it difficult toa sses the country's human trafficking problem or the government's attempts to curb it; NGOs report that laws against human trafficking, froced labor, and debt bondage remain unenforced because of lack of political will and widespread political corruption; there is no evidence that the government has a procses to identify trafficking victims, refers victims to protective services, or has made efforts to prevent human trafficking (2013).

Illicit drugs:

despite substantial interdiction efforts and considerable control measures along the border with Afghanistan, Iran remains one of the primary transshipment routes for Southwest Asian heroin to Europe; suffers one of the highest opiate addiction rates in the world, and has an increasing problem with synthetic drugs; lacks anti-money laundering laws; has reached out to neighboring countries to share counter-drug intelligence

Other Key Facts™ Titles

All Key Facts™ Titles are Available at

www.Amazon.com

THE INTERNATIONALIST®.

http://www.internationalist.com

www.ingramcontent.com/pod-product-compliance
Lightning Source LLC
Chambersburg PA
CBHW051252170526
45165CB00004B/1687